Southwick Long Ago
A collection of memories by Herbert Wing
Edited by
Christine Lawrence

Published by Christine Lawrence
with kind permission from Herbert Wing's family

© Christine Lawrence 2016
The moral right of the author has been asserted

All rights reserved.
No part of this publication may be reproduced, stored in a retrieval system, or transmitted, in any form or by any means without the prior permission in writing of the publisher, nor be otherwise circulated in any form of binding or cover other than in which it is published and without a similar condition including this condition being imposed on the subsequent purchaser.

ISBN - 9781849617

Foreword

Herbert Wing was born in June 1901 in the village of Southwick in Hampshire. He lived in the village for much of his early life, leaving to work in a sports shop in Reading as a young adult. He became an accountant and worked in Reading until he retired at age 65 when he returned to Southwick to live for his remaining years. In July 1980 he began writing his stories of *Southwick Long Ago* which were published in the Parish Newsletter. When he died in 1988, his sister, Edwina, gave permission for these stories to be printed into a small booklet, a copy of which his family now have. As a matter of interest, Edwina is famous for being the barmaid in the Golden Lion at the time of D-Day in 1944 and she often served drinks to Eisenhower and Montgomery.

In 2014, 70 years after D-Day, Southwick Village held a weekend event to commemorate the part that Southwick House and the village had in the D-Day landings. I was lucky enough to have the original copies of Mr. Wing's stories from the Parish Newsletters and being unaware at the time of the original booklet being published I copied all the stories, printed them and scattered them about the tables in the D-Day Memorial Hall so that people could read them whilst enjoying their tea and cakes. Many people asked if they could have copies and this prompted me to take up the challenge of putting them together. I have sought the permission of Mr. Wing's relatives, who kindly have allowed me to go ahead and produce this new publication.

The stories have been printed in the order that they appeared in the Newsletters and are as Mr. Wing originally wrote them. Each story is short, this was due to the limitation placed on him by the Editor of the Newsletter at the time - I am sure he could have said much more if there had been the space. However, they help us to understand what life was like in Southwick in the early part of the 20th Century, describing his boyhood in a village which was then rich in amenities and even included a regular bus service and a thriving school which is more than we have now.

Proceeds from this publication will go towards Southwick Revival charities and improving Southwick Village amenities.

Christine Lawrence

Southwick Long Ago

Whilst having an interesting chat with the Rev. R. Moore on one of his parish visits, our talk turned to days of long ago in the village, and on leaving him he suggested that I penned some of my old memories for insertion in his Parish Newsletter as he thought they would be of interest to some of the "not so old" parishioners.

Naturally the Church formed the main topic of our conversation and I would think that my first connection with 'St. James' would be through the Sunday School about the time I started Day School at 5 years old. Our afternoon lessons, conducted by the local Schoolmaster's wife, were held in the School, but on special occasions we marched over to the Church.

I joined the choir about 3 or 4 years later, in the well-filled gallery, with the younger members down at the front, a line of older girls, and behind them the bigger boys. Further back were the Tenor and Bass men, manly comprised of a well know local farmer, Mr. Albert Parrett of Manor Farm, South Boarhunt, and his several sons.

We always produced an Anthem at Eastertide, accompanied on the old harmonium by our Choirmaster, the local Schoolmaster, which entailed much extra practice. Despite the distance some members had to walk from outside the village, (no public transport in those days) we always got a good attendance and I was reminded of this when meeting a lady recently who, in her earliest teens walked the two miles through narrow lanes and meadow paths from the farm cottage where her family lived. How many girls or young women would risk such a journey in these (supposed) enlightened days?

HJW. (from the Parish Magazine – September 1980)

Southwick Long Ago

I hesitate to plug the often-used cliché of "The Good Old Days", as I know too well that they were anything but that for parents and others on low incomes but I do honestly believe that we youngsters had a happier time than those of today, in the years leading up to the 1914-18 war.

With no television, radio or picture houses to distract us, we had to make our own fun, and "make" was often the operative word. We made our own pop-guns, from stout elder burned through with a red hot poker, plus a ramrod of hazel, with bullets of damp but more often "chewed" paper. Bows also came from hazel sticks with arrows of dead stalks weighted with a cork on the end.

Catapults too were favoured; if a lad was lucky enough to have a few pence to spare he could buy a few inches of quarter-inch square elastic from the local stores, otherwise he had to raid his mother's workbox for possibly some garter elastic. This reads like a lot of lethal weapons but I cannot remember any serious accidents accruing from their use.

Another favourite and beneficial pastime was trolling our hoops, the girls with their wooden ones propelled with a stick, the boys with their faster models of iron with short wire hooks for drive. All were able to use uncluttered village roads until our arch-enemy, the motor car made its appearance to restrict our fun. Of course, we got into plenty of mischief as most boys do but there was not the vandalism as we know it today, nor the mugging of old ladies. In fact, in the main the children were brought up to respect elderly folk, and possibly, feared them. I remember one old lady in particular, whose progeny is still well represented in the district, who only had to look out of her front door when a bunch of us children were making an undue noise outside her house and we would scatter before she had the need to admonish us.

Perhaps we had bigger deterrents in those days – to be involved in a Police Court case was really damaging to your own and your family's local reputation. Also the big village "Bobby", (all policemen were big then), who could sometimes administer his own rough justice; and there were those thick leather belts which most working men wore over their corduroy trousers, (for just what purpose I could never work out, as they were always too slack to help keep them up) but they certainly hurt if you were the victim of a "strapping".

HJW   (From The Parish Magazine May and June 1981)

Southwick Long Ago

Still harking back to boyhood days before the first World War, I was particularly reminded, when watching with horror recently, the greatest fire in the village in my remembrance which almost destroyed Castle Farm, just how much the sporting boys of that era owed to the then tenant farmer, Mr. Edward (Teddy) Palmer.

The Carthouse meadow adjoining the farm was the 'Mecca' for all the village boys interested, any one of whom could go to the farm back door and ask permission to enter the little room just inside, wherein could be found almost any item of equipment needed for any particular game and the summer evenings rang with the shouts and laughter of the two 'pickup' junior cricket teams. Mr Palmer, an ex-cricket captain himself, had two sons who were keen players, and as I was the main pal of the younger, Leslie, from the start of our school days, I was especially privileged and spent all my leisure hours at the farm. I was very sad to see that fine old barn, in which at times we had so much fun, go up in flames.

Next to Castle Farm, I would think that the most likely place to find a bunch of lads together would be down at the old Forge. I can just remember Mr. Page Senior, but he retired and handed over the business to his two sons, William and Robert. The latter branched out on his own after a few years to a forge at Portchester, so Mr. Williams is best remembered as he ran the business for many years before retiring, as I believe, the village's last farrier.

A horse being shod was always fascinating to watch, but the little crowd would increase when word got around that the blacksmith was heating up the iron rims to go over the felloes of wagon or cart wheels. This operation took place in a high narrow brick building at the end of the main one, where the rim would be fired by blazing baffins or untrimmed faggots of rough brushwood and brambles. These had to be renewed several times and our thrills came when the big iron door had to be opened and we saw the blaze going on inside. We usually stayed for the final scene, the red hot rims being taken out of the 'oven' with long iron pincers and burned onto the wheels. I never did really understand how those rims bound and stayed on those wheels after that burning.

Just another delight our village boys are missing today.

HJW   (from the Parish Newsletter January & February 1982)

Southwick Long Ago

In my previous contribution I wrote of the most likely spots for the boys to congregate in my boyhood era, which do not exist as such now but although the men's main link-ups have not changed in venue, the difference in set-up and atmosphere today is considerable.

I refer, of course, to our two public houses, The Red and Golden Lions, the latter taking precedence in that it had a full license and was a Free House and brewed its own beer. The proprietor, a Mr. Harry Hunt, originally lived on the premises, but later moved to a house in Cosham and the responsibility for the management was left to a Miss Brown, a smart, well-built lady who owned a parrot well-versed in 'Bar Language', and a snappy little dog called Dinky.

The public bar then was a widened out centre of the passage that ran from front to back entrance, stone floored, with a narrow sawdust spittoon running along the bar base. Also a long wooden seat was at the back which was seldom used. To the left of the bar was a private room, used mainly by local farmers, business men, or better-paid work folk, who probably paid tuppence ha'penny per pint of beer against the tuppence in the public side. I never learned spirit prices. The long oblong room, now the public bar, was only used on national celebrations, or as the climax to Old Club days, for an impromptu dance.

But the mainstay of the business was undoubtably Mr. R. (Dick) Olding, who spent most of his working life there as a gardener, sometimes stand-in manager, and more importantly as brewer, until almost the end of his life. All the village knew when Dick was brewing, as the smell of the steaming hops pervaded the atmosphere, which like the brew, was not always appreciated – the local 'swillers' being divided in opinion on taste and quality – but the 'Home Brew' gained a good reputation over a wide area, especially with the arrival of the motor car for travel.

The Red Lion, then a beer house, had its devotees, preferring the beer as supplied by the Portsmouth United Breweries, sold by landlord Mr. T. (Darkie) Ainsworth, who took over the license after being badly crippled by an accident when working on the railways. Like his son, William, of whom I have previously written, he was a jocular type of man and loved 'putting one over' on his customers at times, so they took delight in catching him out. Apart from his refreshment business, he and his son provided the only local transport for all occasions with his horse and carriage. The Red Lion, now fully licensed, has been modernised, but changed little in structure from those early days.

Bad old days? Beer tuppence a pint – 4.5 gallon cask four shillings and sixpence, delivered. - What now?

HJW   (from the Parish Newsletter May 1982)

Southwick Long Ago

Further to my previous contribution and the story of the late "Old Post Office Stores", in the early years, a slice of village history was lost when the old building was converted to a private dwelling. The old granary and outhouses still stand I believe, but the possible most interesting part, the bakehouse, disappeared. I assume that the 'Faithfull' family baked and sold bread in their early take-over years, but I do know that the big brick oven, with its stout iron door, was regularly used by the villagers, who brought their one joint of meat per week to be baked for their Sunday dinner, at the costly fee of threepence a time.

When discussing the family history with a very elderly cousin, just after the death of the last member (Horace), he told me that Mr. Faithfull senior was mainly interested in breeding and buying-in pigs for slaughter, and used to take half carcasses to Portsmouth in his horse-drawn cart for sale to Port Butchers, etc., the said relative accompanying him to look after the horses.

I cannot remember seeing the outfit but in my memory time pigs and port were very much to the fore-front of home trade at the shop, a 4 – 5 score pig being regularly killed and dressed on the premises and the astute Mrs. Faithfull saw to it that nothing was wasted, the offal being turned into brawn, chitterlings and scarps (the latter to me always looked a mess of indigestible fat), but all sold well and added a cheap addition to a meal.

During my conversation with the family cousin, he told me an extraordinary story concerning Charles during the first World War. Both Arthur the elder and Horace the younger brother had joined the Services, but Charles claimed exemption on the grounds that his job as Post Officer was essential. The tribunal allowed him six months grace on the first appeal, but after that he was called to the Colours, so with his railway warrant plus his small case, he bid farewell to his mother to walk over the hill to Portchester station only to find that, owing to a strike or other disruption no trains were running, so he was back home within an hour. Asked what he was going to do next, he replied "Wait for another call." But apparently the War or Records Offices lost track of him, as he never heard from them again. On reflection, I wondered how often this might have happened nationally.

HJW   (from the Parish Newsletter   Winter 1982)

Southwick Long Ago

Further to my contributions on the village amenities in the early days of the century, we had a resident fishmonger, a Mr Roberts, who arrived in the village towards the end of the first decade and rented what is now known as 'The White House', in the High Street, where he had stabling for his two working ponies. One of these did the early morning journey down to the Portsmouth Fish Market, whilst the second was harnessed up for the day's selling round.

I believe Mr. Roberts served his local and district customers about three days a week, covering the village at first, then up through the Southwick Common to Newtown, Worlds End, and taking in outlying farms and isolated cottages en route. Trading was good, as fish was no doubt the cheapest flesh food obtainable, and cash was very tight those days.

Those ponies in the stables were the main attraction for me in getting myself ingratiated with the Roberts family, and in no time I was cantering one of them through the village from the hired grazing meadow off the Back Lane, and although I had little control with only a hemp halter and single rein, there was little likelihood of meeting any traffic either than the local carrier's horse and van.

Mr. Roberts was also a popular purveyor on Southwick Fair and Old Club days, running a whelk stall and selling bumper oranges at at penny a time. Another decided acquisition to the village was having a local shoe mender, a Mr. C. (Charlie) Green, whose home and workshop was the last cottage on the bank in West Street, (now tenanted by Mr. Tomlin). Here one entered the side gate, walked along a garden path to a wooden hutment, where on entry, one was met by a lovely smell of leather and beeswax, plus a cheerful smile from Mr. G., who never seemed ruffled by anything, and that despite the handicap of his own permanent lameness, plus a badly crippled invalid brother lying in a portable bed/chair in the warm room.

    Charlie was a very articulate countryman and a real philosopher and although being only a 'nipper' when I used to take my scuffed-out shoes for 'doctoring', I used to be fascinated by his stories and view on life. He had a good business, his clientele including the young squire (as the locals termed the gentleman from the mansion), but he never made a fortune and never wished to, as he expressed to friends in later life. Sports-wise, he loved cricket, and post-war never missed a match in Park Meadow, joining the critical 'oldies' on the pavilion bench. A man content with his life.

HJW   (from the Parish Newsletter Spring 1983)

Southwick Long Ago

Probably the biggest blow to the local community up to the 1914 War was the loss of a 'resident' doctor, and although it was rumoured that the last one to leave might return after War Service, it was not to be. I think he decided that the practice was no longer viable financially. I don't know how far back our 'medicine men' went, but the three in my time were a Dr. Rundle, who was probably here at the turn of the century, a Dr. Clarke-Baylis, and last but not least, a Dr. Balthazar. Each of these gentlemen lived and held surgery at what is now called "South Lodge", the first named probably leaving about 1905. Dr. Baylis followed, but was only around for a very few years and was not very highly thought of locally in the medical sense I believe.

Certainly the village folk were stunned when the news spread one day that he had died suddenly that morning, as he had been seen the previous day on his rounds. The rumour spread that the cause of death was blood poisoning, due to a cat's scratch but I think I am right in stating that there was no public enquiry and no official statement issued. Mystery was added to the tragedy by a rumour that there was domestic trouble at the Doctor's house (as the residency was generally known) but I was too young to fully understand the implications suggested.

Dr. Balthazar, a young man with updated medical ideas, though not always sympathetic or attentive to minor ailments, was generally credited with giving his full attention and interest in any patient seriously ill, and one in particular, an eldest son of a well-known local family, always declared that Dr. B. saved his life, when seriously ill with Bronchial-Pneumonia (a killer in those days). The good doctor practically lived in his cottage for 48 hours until the crisis had passed.

The war came, with younger fit doctors soon in much demand by the Services, so Dr. Balthazar took a commission in the RAMC and went off to war. Not long afterwards his attractive wife and pretty little daughter, Minky, left to live in Brighton and that was the end of the 'Doctor's House' as such. It also started the era of the visiting Doctor, (still in vogue, but mercifully in larger premises), the first Surgery being held in one of the smallest houses in the village, (since joined with the house next door to form a reasonable dwelling), the waiting room in the kitchen with the family (if room), the Doctor's ill-lit room adjoining.

HJW (from the Parish Newsletter Summer 1983)

Editor's note: Southwick no longer has a visiting Doctor, unfortunately this service has gone the same way as the buses.

Southwick Long Ago

In earlier contributions I have listed some local 'Good Men and True' who helped to keep the old village ticking over. I switch now to a local character who, for most of his time, was very much in the opposite category. I refer to one George, better remembered by all who know of him as Fash, who lived somewhere in the district with his mother in early life.

A very introverted lad apparently, he was nicknamed 'Old Fashioned' early on but this was later streamlined to Fash and he was known as such in many districts around. As a youth he had distinguished himself by stopping a young girl in local service from committing suicide, by pulling her out of a river or pond, for which he was awarded a watch, I believe, by the Royal Humane Society.

After the death of his mother he turned to vagrancy, sleeping rough mainly in local farm outbuildings, whilst generally working on the farm concerned, receiving in lieu his food and perhaps a shilling at the end of the week. Fash was a skilled worker in all land work, but he continually 'queered his pitch' by blowing his wages (6 pints of strong ale for a shilling), in one of the district public houses, which meant that he had no money left for his addiction to strong liquor. This led him into crime by theft, mainly of farm tools or vegetables, etc., to sell, sometimes from the farm which had been sheltering him, which my mother used to call 'biting the hand that fed him'.

Although these thefts seldom brought in more than a few shillings, they were usually reported to the local 'arm of the law', the village Bobby, whose job then was to march his prisoner into Fareham Police Station and an appearance before the bench later always meant a month or two 'holidays' in Kingston Prison. One arrest in particular caused much amusement. Sometime around 1910 we had a new village constable, a big fellow called Dymes, who had hardly settled in before he had to take the long walk with Fash. At the second high stile on the then well-worn path, across the fields, Fash stood aside saying "After you Sir", and the new PC, thinking it a polite gesture, climbed over, only to see his charge disappearing down the track towards Ham Farm and copse, and it was two days before he could pick him up again.

My reference to a prison 'holiday' was apt in Fash's case, as he got much benefit from it, being treated as a 'Trusty' and allowed to work in the prison gardens daily, he was sure of his food, was cleaned up and sent out as a (temporary) respectable citizen. Having raked out the Fash file from my memory bank, I find there are so many little anecdotes untold, that I may continue his story in my next Newsletter contribution.

HJW (from the Parish Newsletter   Winter 1983)

Southwick Long Ago

Several readers of my last newsletter article expressed interest in my attempted biography of 'Old Fash', and I am indebted to Mrs. Mabel Long, who kindly turned over her old photographs and loaned me a postcard picture of our old 'vagrant' possibly the only pictorial record of him in existence. Taken. I believe, about 1925, outside the Red Lion, it depicted the farm staff of the late of the late Mr. Bertram Crook, with his son Percy (happily still with us) plus Mr. Albert Leppard and Mr. Charlie Stubbs (like Fash, no longer existent), with Fash making up the line. Roughly clad, and looking smaller than I had imagined, he had removed his hat to reveal a very grey head and beard, but well trimmed, and his keen look belied his mode of living.

Stories of his exploits are legion and to understand the more outrageous, one has to know that, approaching middle-age he had developed a shakiness of hands and voice, and become somewhat more scruffy, so some landlords around the district were refusing to serve him on the grounds that some of their customers objected to his company. But Fash had to have his pinta somehow, and on one famous occasion when refused, said he would help himself, whereupon he opened his shirt and released a small swarm of bees, which cleared the bar whilst he drew himself a free drink.

On another occasion, again with a bulging shirt, he was asked what was moving inside, and promptly produced a pet rat. A gamekeeper there who had a couple of ferrets with him, offered him a pint if he would put one of the ferrets inside with the rat. Fash obliged, and when the squeaking and scrambling around his waist was over, he enjoyed another free drink.

In case the reader of the first story thinks it sounds a bit far fetched, I can personally vouch for Fash's affinity with the bees, as when coming up the Back Lane one warm day in May, I espied a lovely swarm just settling on a short hedge on a bank, and had ideas of making some quick pocket money by informing the Estate head gardener, Mr. Gilbert, of its location. Alas for my hopes, the old fox had tracked them, had got himself a cardboard box, and was lifting them into it, and with no protection whatsoever, the insects crawling over his bare arms and hands. I kept my distance but could see no signs of emotion as he flicked the stray ones into the box. Five shillings well earned, but I must leave his story here with much untold as I am running out of allotted space, except to state that he spent the last few years of his life with another 'down-and-out' friend for company in a farm outbuilding in World's End.

HJW   (from the Parish Newsletter   January 1984)

Southwick Long Ago

I was especially interested in reading our last Newsletter which I would think was our best so far for interest and information, and I marvelled at the number of warmhearted people in the district who give their time and energy towards giving pleasure and help to all and sundry from young children to oldies like myself.

I was particularly interested in the long contribution on the First Southwick Brownie and Cub Pack which took my memory back to early 1911, when the late Colonel Borthwick attempted to form a Southwick Scout Pack. Our schoolboys had been informed of his intended visit by our schoolmaster, Mr. F. J. Mowlem, who gave us some of the possible interests in scouting, suggesting that, as we would be supplied with wooden staves, we could made 'Big Dandy' an enemy and chase him over the Downs, Big Dandy being the biggest lad in the school by far and the elder son of the then tenant of Pigeonhouse Farm.

The well-intentioned Colonel duly came into school one afternoon and gave us the low-down on scouting, then asking for a 'hands-up' as to how many boys would like to join the venture. I was interested through reading of the fairly new Scout Movement, so my hand went up right away, but unfortunately it was the only one raised, so a grand offer fizzled out.

In the Jan/Feb issue (1983) of the Newsletter, a letter from a Mr. B.S.Compton to the Rev Moore appeared and in an addendum below his signature he mentioned a local character who should have been included in my writings on St. James' Church notabilities, the well-known sexton for many years, a Mr. Tommy Horton. A tiny little man, who came from the Isle-of-Wight, he was best known by the Church-goers for his loud responses from the little pew under the pulpit, always a second in front of the congregation, in the Lords Prayer and the Amens. Among his varied jobs, he rang the bell for services, the Knell, for a death, and was credited with ringing the only three bells useable in the annual peal on Christmas Eve.

Tommy, a widower I believe when he came to the village, lived with his daughter Nellie, who looked after him and the Church and always wore a black dress and a black straw Boater hat. Apart from his Church duties, Tommy worked in the Estate forestry nursery, and I was privileged to watch him on several occasions, making the much-used birch brooms, and to listen to his boyhood tales of life in the Island.

HJW (from the Parish Newsletter May/May 1984)

Southwick Long Ago

In the last issue of the Newsletter, two printing errors may have proved misleading to some readers. Firstly, in my story of Colonel Borthwick's attempt to form a Scout Group in 1911, and our Schoolmaster's jocular remark about chasing 'Big Dandy', it should have read 'with wooden staves', not stoves. Later, in my reference to Mr. (Tommy) Horton, his position was as Sexton not Secotr.

    A while back I saw on the television a collection of old farm carts, amongst them one of the open type four wheel vans I mentioned in an early article, as supplied by district market gardeners to take us children on our annual outing to Southsea. I got to wondering whether there were still any of that class around in Boarhunt, Newton, Soberton districts. I well remember lying awake, occasionally listening to the clip-clop of the horses' hooves as they wended their way on our hard stone High Street (usually, I believe, between 1 and 2 am) taking the loads of vegetables, fruit, etc. to their Portsmouth market stands. Hours later, generally early afternoon, they would be drifting back, and on a warm afternoon, it was not unusual to see several 'drivers' fast asleep, their tired but well trained horses taking them home at their own steady pace.
    Sometimes a younger fresh horse had to be brought in who did not 'know the ropes', and one such, with driver asleep, followed the van in front (driver awake), out of the village on the wrong track. For a lark the front man decided to leave things as they were until after a few miles he pulled up to ask his colleague at the back if he was taking a trip around the countryside. His now awakened friend's reply is unprintable.
    On an evening off, sometimes a marketeer would harness up to a two-wheeled trap to visit a pub or friends. One who was a regular visitor to the village had overstayed

his usual time and was approaching Staple Cross near the midnight hour on his way home. There was a sudden rattling of chains, the shafts shot up and the horse bolted, the driver declaring that the Devil himself had jumped on the back of the trap, frightening horse and driver. More sombre-minded friends decided that a fox crossing the road, dragging a gin-trap, was the more likely culprit.

Apparently Staple Cross always had a spooky history, as I learned from an old uncle, who was walking back from a late session at Boarhunt and had reached the line of oak trees which then lined the road leading to the 'Cross', when he heard movements in front. He stopped, they stopped, and finally he rushed forward and hit out with his stick, only to land on the back of an old sow gathering acorns. The roar that followed near frightened him to death!

HJW   (from the Parish Newsletter June/August 1984)

Southwick Long Ago

Still ruminating on the joys of living in the early century for a village lad, one of the big excitements for me was seeing a horse-drawn fire-engine for the first time. This came about through a fire which had started up in a dressing room at Oak Lodge House (now The Oaks), where the Honourable Mrs. Long had been changing her attire prior to going out. Mrs. Long was one of a minority of ladies who smoked cigarettes in those days, and had apparently left one on her dressing table still burning when she left the room.

With no telephone communication available and the motorcar yet to arrive at Oak Lodge, it was left to the groom, a Mr. Harry Sutton, to saddle up. Harry might have created a record for the full distance had he not been unlucky in that his horse slipped up and both horse and rider came a 'purler' on the hard stone road at Wallington, and Harry, already dazed and excited, was yelling to folks who soon assembled, "Mr Guvnor's house is on fire, somebody fetch the Fire Brigade." Someone evidently obliged and contacted the Fire Chief, who then had to collect his part-time firemen and order the horses from the contractors, M/S Dyke of Fareham.

Meanwhile, I had arrived home from afternoon school, around 3.30, and been told by my Mother of the fire and that Mr. Sutton had gone to Fareham to fetch the Fire Brigade. Also that I was not to go near the outbreak. But I had seen pictures of galloping steeds and their outfit on the way to fires, and the chance now to see them for real was just too strong a temptation. So for once I disobeyed her and slunk off down to the bottom of West Street. I had not long to wait before I heard the clatter of the fire-fighting outfit coming down the Ham Hill, and then the grand sight as it rounded the curve of the Old Fareham Road and over Cheeseman's Bridge at the gallop, with the engine bell at full clang, a never-to-be-forgotten thrill for a horse-mad youngster.

Of the fire itself, I remember little, as I partly obeyed

parental orders in not going closer than the tall line of trees where I was hiding. I think it was confined mainly to the one room, which was just as well as it must have been all of an hour between alarm being raised and 'professionals' arrival. What a hope for a *big* country house fire in those days!

HJW   (from the Parish Newsletter Winter 1984)

Southwick Long Ago

I was very pleased to read in our local newspaper that the old village Forge has come to life again, Mr. Gladwell having found a sub-tenant in a Mr. Dave Cox from Horndean, who can claim connection with the village through his Grandma being born here, and his Great-Grandfather was a gamekeeper on the Southwick Estate. The lady responsible for the article started it with "The sound of hammer on anvil is echoing through Southwick once more" - but not with the volume I first remember, when there was practically no traffic noise to smother it, and particularly when blacksmith Mr. Will Page and his assistant were working overtime during the winter months.

This late working led to the apprentice, a local boy taken on as a school-leaver, getting the nick-name of 'Tinker Moonshine'. Young Frank was not tall, but certainly thick-set and a few years of swinging the big hammer soon put some muscle on him, but he got the wander-lust and went away to Australia where he married and settled down.

Seeing the roadside torn up at the top of West street a short while back, and learning that there was some trouble with the water-piping, I got to wondering what some of the young to middle-aged housewives would have thought of the often hard work it was to obtain sufficient water for their daily needs, by their counterparts up to 1921.

With the exception of the few larger houses which had inside pumps, there were few outside ones and these had to be shared, the most notable being the 'Village Pump' on the green, which supplied a number of homes near-by. Otherwise it was the old type cottage well, which looks picturesque when 'dummied' in present day gardens but meant some daily heavy work when in use, especially for a woman. Apart from the jagged and broken ropes and deterioration of timber at the top, there could be trouble in the well itself, silting up, and worse still, bricks caving in to cause blockage and endanger the life of any man going down or working in the confined space.

I remember watching an elderly man preparing to descend a cottage well, who produced a ball of stout string to which he attached a lighted candle which was lowered into the hole to test for gas. The candle returned still alight so apparently all was well.

Buckets breaking adrift often, and I remember a story current at the time, of two local men calling on a friend outside the village who was using a grab-hook to retrieve his bucket. Conversation thus - "Lost your bucket Bill?"

"No, it ain't lost. It's down the well."

Illogical perhaps, but I think Bill had a point.

HJW   (from the Parish Newsletter January/February 1985)

Southwick Long Ago

Every few weeks I drive over the Portsdown Hill to Cosham, to obtain some cash and to buy a few necessary items, and have several times thought how different the general layout of the journey looks from my first early Century trips.

For a start, I wonder how many of our village folk have seen or even know there was an 18 hole golf course stretching along the Downs on our side of the hills. It started at the Club House, just below Widley Fort on the North side, the first 'hole' running downhill to number one green just above the fence enclosing the farming land below. After this the course ran due West on the lower Downland to above the New Barns Farmland, turning back over the higher part of the hill to finish on the 18th near the Club House.

I have forgotten the club's title but I believe it was patronised mainly by Service Officers and top business men from Portsmouth and around. Like so many other things it closed down in 1914, and incidentally killed my hopes of a possible apprenticeship later which might have altered my working life considerably, in-as-much as the professional at the club, a Mr. Morris, had offered me a job under him when later I left school.

Unfortunately the War not only killed the Club, but its young 'Pro' as well, he having joined up early and given his life for his country. One of the notable local golf ladies was Mrs. Balthazar, the pretty wife of our last resident doctor. I used to visit her home, now South Lodge, after school hours to do odd jobs, including cleaning her golf clubs, and when she had a special game to play, usually a monthly spoon competition she would take me along to caddy for her. This generally happened in midweek, and meant that I had to play truant from school. I used to keep out of sight until after 1.30pm then skip up the road and away in her tiny three-wheeled car. After her round Mrs. B. and male partner would spend a while in the Clubhouse, whilst I made a line to the 'pros' shop, where I used to do some more club cleaning, an eternal job with irons all of plain steel. This was how I came to know Mr. Morris.

I already had an interest in the game when very young as I was lent a specially made miniature set of clubs by an older cousin and played along the edge of the Hayling Links while he was out on the course, but a number of years passed before I was able to be actively involved in the game, mainly on Berkshire courses.

HJW   (from the Parish Newsletter March/May 1985)

Southwick Long Ago

A few weeks back, when down at the bottom of our garden, I was buzzed by a large insect and when I had fenced it off, I realised that it was a Hornet, the first I had seen for many years and it brought me back to my theme in our last newsletter, the changed face of our patch of the South Downs from earlier days.

There were a number of thorn bushes scattered about the Hill and on the right of the road about where the entrance to ARE is now was a large bush which always seemed to house a swarm of hornets, which we boys used to tease, and then had to run away quick to escape being stung.

One pleasant night during summer days was a flock of sheep grazing happily in the sun, this flock belonging to the tenant farmer of Offwell and New Barns Farms. Not so noticeable was a smaller flock to the East which came from Pigeonhouse Farm, and I was reminded of that by remembering a rather rural story which circulated concerning it.

The farmer owner had a habit of adding a suffix to questions or observations he made of "Look, I means...", and one day when his two sons plus a nephew were pitching fresh pens for the fattening lambs, one of the early large ones was persistently jumping over the previous pen 'gate', for, it seems, as our American friends would put it, "just for the hell of it". The farmer's nephew decided to stop his gallop, so arming himself with a hurdle shore, he crouched down by the side of the gate, and when the offending animal came over, swung his pole too lustily, hitting the poor lamb on the head and killing it. This meant facing Uncle with the bad news, when the ensuing conversation went like this:-

    Nephew: I'm very sorry Uncle.
    Uncle: Very sorry, look I means.
    Nephew: I didn't mean to kill him, Uncle.
    Uncle: Didn't mean to kill him, look I means.

Nephew: It was only a shore, Uncle.
Uncle: Only a shore, look I means.
Nephew: But I didn't hit him very hard Uncle.
Uncle: Hard enough to kill him, look I means.

I do not remember the farmer concerned all that well, as he did not seem to visit the village much but one pleasing reminder of him was of a couple or more visits on a Friday evening with horse and cart to pick up bags of acorns for feeding to his pigs, which local youngsters collected after school and at weekends, for which he paid sixpence per bushel.

HJW (from The Parish Newsletter, Summer 1985)

Southwick Long Ago

When reading some of the history of the 'Royals' a while back, I realised that in recording our 'special' days of the early century, I had omitted a very grand one, the Coronation Day of King George the fifth, which was celebrated throughout the land in 1911.

If I remember rightly, the day's enjoyment started in the old Oak Meadow, with the children's sports, and I certainly recall that it started for me with first elation and then sudden disappointment. Notices about the races and other events appeared several weeks before, so we budding 'Seb Coes' got down to practice, especially for the three-legged race, which was always a favourite. I had teamed up with a local lad about a couple of years older than myself, and we made a good and fast pair.

The big day came, and only a short while before we have to line up, my 'other half' informed me that he intended to run with another local lad about his own age – I was upset and annoyed, but just before 'call-up', I spied a friend arriving, one George Parrett, one of the sons of the well-known local farming family. I begged him to run with me, which he agreed. We lined up with the 'field', and one of the local men stewards tied our ankles together with my best Sunday hanky, and we were off. I struck up an easy rhythm with George and we ran out the winners. But our elation only lasted about 10 minutes when we were called back, a local objector declaring that some hankies were tied tighter than others.

On the second run and tie-up, I was told to push my leg tighter to my partner's and as soon as I moved the tie was pulled tight with my right toes onto my partner's left foot, so I was tripping him from the start and we finished in a heap after a dozen yards or so.

Apparently, Oak Meadow was not convenient to hold the tea tent (no piped water about then), so a marquee was erected in the Golden Lion yard for our 'Bun Fight', and we had a good feast, each child receiving a well-made and decorated Coronation Mug.

No band available, but the late Mr. Arthur S. Faithful kindly enlivened the party by fetching his concertina, and got us kids singing and dancing for a couple of hours.

For generations Children's Races have been one of the main attractions at village fetes and carnivals, as it covers the whole watching population age-wise, the proud Mums and Grandmas with their competing toddlers, the school pals cheering on their mates and perhaps some senior races thrown in. It seems to have lost favour locally the last few years since Mr. Frank Harvey used to organise a series of races from tots to teens for many years.

HJW   (from the Parish Newsletter January/February 1986)

Southwick Long Ago

With Christmastide over and a New Year in prospect, I had made mental notes of the possible format of my next contribution to the newsletter due in mid February, but by that time I was in no mental or physical condition to oblige, so it was heartening to read the over-eulogistic remarks on my previous efforts when the February copy came out.

I had mentally planned after Xmas to use my forthcoming contribution as a means to say thank you for several blessings enjoyed: the Bell-Ringers' efforts, the Sunday evening of Carols, the annual distribution of logs and Xmas pudding by HMS Dryad, and especially the gifts for us oldies from the Youth Club. The young blonde girl who knocked our door was so obviously happy in handing in the gift made it all the more acceptable. What a bonus for our country's future if there are more people willing to give up their spare time to train young folk to think of others and be the better citizens of tomorrow.

Still thinking of Xmas gifts, a young relative gave me some very interesting reading, a book titled "The Hampshire Village Book", covering some 135 villages and districts in 185 pages of potted histories and customs of the villages noted, which I would recommend to any reader of country folklore. I was a bit peeved that Southwick was omitted, (our near-neighbour's villages got a good write-up), as I am sure that our village will figure more prominently in the history books of the future.

The fore-word to the book above was written by my favourite writer and broadcaster on rural life, John Arlott, who in suggesting the Author is all but too late in portraying the true village life, states,

"It is within living memory that villages were busy places, the smoke of the fire, the wheeze of the bellows, thud or hammers and smell of burning hooves came from the smithy. On

Mondays cottage gardens were whitely plentiful with washing, with housewives bustling out to the clothes line and back to a kitchen from which came the smell of cooking, especially boiling bacon or baking cakes. The back garden held its pig, if all was well, with a litter, a cluck-chattering chicken run and enough cabbage and potatoes to last the best part of the year round and a couple of elderly apple trees."

    A typical picture of an elderly Uncle's cottage at the North end of the High Street, but that must be another story.
HJW   (from the Parish Newsletter Summer 1986)

Southwick Long Ago

In my previous contribution I finished by quoting John Arlott's foreword to the Hampshire Village Book on village life and conditions early in the century, and I considered his description typical of an elderly uncle's cottage and life at the north end of the High Street.

I met the little lady a while back who is now the tenant of no. 46. I told her of my particular interest going back to the first decade, and she gave me carte blanche to look in at any time on what was my second home up until the early 1920s, but, alas, on my visit this day, there was hardly anything to stir my memory of the good old days. Almost everything had changed. Old Uncle Philip was the hardest working man I ever knew, building his pigsties, rabbit breeding hutches, chicken run, etc., and working a strip of 40 rod length in the Berry Allotments, 14 more in the smaller patch opposite the Red Lion, plus a long garden stretching up to the Park wall, so there were always plenty of cabbages and potatoes, plus mangels, sweet-corn, etc., to feed both house and animals.

Yes, there was always a breeding sow in the sty with her bunch of piglets in due season, usually around twelve in number, which were sold when six weeks old, fetching about eighteen shillings to one pound each. The large rabbit hutches were alive with youngsters as several does were kept, these mainly being sold off when a month old at the princely sum of four pence each, and the cluck-chattering chicken run under the Park wall housed a dog and more hens. Yes, and there was even a couple of elderly apple trees, one with an enormous spread which had gone un-pruned for many a year but produced bushels of large fruit every season. Auntie Bess was a good cake maker, and port and boiled bacon were regularly on the menu.

Altogether, I think, endorsing Arlott's description of a real old country cottage.

In my short inspection of the back of the cottages on

the corner, I found that number 47 had been extended, but number 46 had changed but little externally. I don't know if there is a conservation order on the cottage but there should be. I gazed at the building with a fresh interest and could not make up my mind whether it was an architects dream or a nightmare. I don't know of any other village cottage walls enclosed in tessellated tiling, (very decorative), and the jutting out rooms from the centre suggests additions as they went along whilst the view on the north side is imposing. I would like to know if the Conservation people had inspected it and of their report.

HJW   (from the Parish Newsletter Oct/Nov 1986)

Southwick Long Ago

I got to wondering how many local folk interested have been watching the short films on television the last few Sunday evenings. Titled '70 Summers' and narrated by an elderly farmer on the change in farming methods since early century, and especially on the tools and machinery used, from the big Shire Horse to Steam Engine to Tractor to the present day farming wonder, Combine Harvester. I have been lucky in seeing all these changes as they developed and was sometimes involved with some of the earliest ones. I was extra pleased when a very rural retired farm worker, who I would think was about 12 months younger than myself, was brought into the narrative, and, like myself, could carry his story back to before 1914 and the First World War.

In an amusing way, he told how he first started his farming career, when 'some feller' came to his school one day examining the registers and said to him, 'I see you have a good attendance record and have passed the sixth standard, so you can leave school if you wish.' The old boy apparently did not need a second invitation and was off to work the following week. This was possibly in 1914, when war preparations were lessening the manpower available.

I was let off schooling during the summers of 1913 and 1914 to do farm work, returning from the second session on October 1st, then passing a Labour Examination in a Fareham school at the end of that month and I was free of the classroom again. I doubt if I got as much joy over leaving as the old chap mentioned above apparently felt, as school work seldom bothered me. Perhaps I was more concerned about the wage packet I had recently lost of 4 shillings per week towards the family budget.

I don't know whether the disease known as Scarlet Fever still exists, but in my schooldays it visited the village on several occasions and the victims (mainly children) were quickly whisked off to the Isolation Hospital for six weeks (in

Fareham). One such epidemic gave me a start in weekly wage earning, as I found a job during the period March to April 1912 as a human scarecrow (or Rook Starver as the farm men called us), keeping the big birds off the up-coming corn, seven days a week at sixpence a day. I made myself a drum out of a large size toffee tin, and aided by a strong, raucous voice, kept the feathered thieves at bay.

HJW   (from the Parish Newsletter   Spring 1987)

Southwick Long Ago

Many old photographs and accounts of happenings (mainly in Portsmouth and around) of before the 1914 war have appeared in the local 'News' in the last few months have have set me thinking back that despite the fact that HMS Dryad undoubtably put our old village on the map of history in the second conflict (1939/45), Southwick had connections with the military side in 1914/18 which are little know by locals today, as the menfolk concerned have 'passed on', leaving only a few family ties behind.

I wonder if many folk can realise, when looking up at the Forts still lining the hill, that in 1914, those same forts house the might of England's heavy artillery, the 26th - 35th & 108th Batteries, of guns hauled by eight heave horses, all we could muster at the outset to send to France?

Although I believe that we were badly prepared, no doubt we had some spare guns and vehicles in reserve, but horses? That was a different matter and I well remember one July 1914 afternoon when the lower end of the High Street was filled with about 25 or more nags, attended by about half a dozen young soldiers, whilst the rest of their mates were bringing out pints of beer from The Red Lion and laughing at rumours of war.

Most of these animals were from local farms, the W.D. Chiefs having sent out assessors to commandeer ones considered suitable, but some amusement was caused among the carters as to the recruits taken, such as Old Joe, a half-legged nippy sort but well into his twenties, or Prince, who had something wrong with his water-works and would be stopping every 100 yards.

But not all were 'duds' and there was a possible prize at Wanstead Farm if the predators had been allowed to see him. A fine upstanding colt named Magnet, from a very ordinary mare but sired by the Fareham & Hants Farmers Club travelling stallion, of which he was a fine copy.

Carrying all the markings and feathering of the fine Shire breed, he was also the pride and joy of his owner, the late Squire, Mr. Alex Thistlethwaite, who gave orders that he was not to be recruited, so he was whisked away from Wanstead to a small stable in the Park until danger passed.

Another piece of duplicity, again involving Wanstead, concerned two new sets of harness, recently bought. They were buried in corn grain in a mew of the granary, in case they should also attract unwanted attention.

HJW   (From the Parish Newsletter Summer 1987)

Southwick Long Ago

I am reminded that the current issue of the Newsletter covers the Christmastide with all its fun. Noting the junior cyclists, mostly girls, on their smart little bikes racing up and down outside on our Castle Road 'racetrack', reminds me that their number will undoubtedly be added to by the 26th December. These additional machines will no doubt require Santa Claus to be reimbursed by £20 and upwards in payments.

My mind wanders back to the first decade of the 20th Century and to my happy Christmases during that period, when inexpensive gifts probably cost less than £5 for the several of us children in the family at that time. I think I was having doubts about the 'nationality' of Santa Claus by the time I started school and thus decided to stay awake long enough on the big night to dispel them. Like many before me I did not manage to stick it out by the time the welcome intruder crept in. Nor was I to do so for by Xmas 1909 we had lost my father, so I became the 'man of the house' and had to be part of the Santa myth for my younger sisters' benefit. And what tiring work it proved to be, with me, Mother and my late elder sister setting off mid-morning to climb that daunting Portsdown Hill, often in bad weather, then a welcome rest inside the old noisy tram on our way into town. The rest of the day was spent traipsing around Pompey to find the gifts to suit specific ages, at a price my Mother's shrinking purse could stand. I don't think I was very helpful as far as selection was concerned (except for the carrying part), as all the toy and sports shops seemed to have a train circulating its window display. These always fascinated me, and meant some back-tracking from my folks to join me in the 'squad' again.

I will always remember best the old Commercial Road before the 'Gerries' smashed it up, especially the golden glow from the jewellers, H. Samuel, (recently sold), seeming to light up half the main street. Additionally there was our one-stop for refreshment early afternoon at the 'Sailor's Rest'! Here two sausages and mash cost 4d. And a rice pudding 2d, a nicely cooked and tasty meal for any travel hungry, long-distance shopper.

By teatime we had to be thinking about getting home and the drag back over the hill (over-loaded with parcels) in the dark. There were no lights of any sort on the village side of the Portsdown Hill in those days, except perhaps when a gypsy family was camped up in the warm dell. Their presence would be forcibly announced if their lurcher dog gave a few barks as we passed. On the other hand, they never came out or interfered with anyone, just sat around their log fire and I don't remember hearing of any molestation resulting from their presence. Southwick at last, a welcome cup of tea and food after which it was necessary to get the younger girls off to bed while we made up the various stockings. (Mother's old ones). After a suitable delay it was necessary to creep about to make sure all the recipients were in the land of 'Nod'. Thus you were lucky to get to bed before the early hours of the 25th, only to be awakened at dawn by the yells of the young voices that 'He' had come. I doubt whether there are many modern parents who work so hard for their children's Xmas pleasure as described above.

HJW (from Parish Newsletter December 87 Jan/Feb 1988)

Herbert James Wing's address
Born June 1901.   Funeral 5th April 1988, burial Boarhunt.

It was in July 1980 that Herbert Wing agreed to write for the Parish Newsletter his stories of Southwick Long Ago. The result is that we have snippets of his long life interwoven with the history of Southwick where he was born. Edwina has given permission for these to be printed in a small booklet, which could be available later this year.

His last contribution was about Christmas. 'By Xmas 1909 we had lost my father, so I became "man of the house (he was then 8 years old), and had to be part of the Santa myth for my younger sisters' benefit." Then followed the story of Christmas shopping in Portsmouth and a stop for refreshment at the Sailors' Rest (where incidentally I signed the pledge, since broken). 'Here', said Bert, '2 sausages and mash cost 4d. and rice pudding 2d.'

He enjoyed his boyhood before World War I and spent much of his leisure time at Castle Farm where the tenant farmer, Teddy Palmer, would store in a little room, the sports equipment for the junior cricket team. The boys made their own fun:- pop-guns from stout alder, with a ramrod of hazel, and bullets of chewed paper.

He spoke of amenities in the village - two shops, 4 visiting bakers, a visiting butcher, resident fishmonger, cobbler and doctor.

Herbert Wing might have become a golf professional. Before working at Wanstead Farm and later with the Estate Agent at Bridge House, he had been offered a job at the 18 hole gold course which spread down Portsdown Hill to Cosham. Unfortunately this closed in 1914 but his interest continued when he went to work at a relative's sports shop in Reading and became actively involved with golf on the Berkshire Downs.

His story has ended, so we must continue it. It was in

Reading that he became Chief Accountant with Gascoines, makers of dairy equipment, retiring at 65.

Then back he came to his native Southwick to live with and be lovingly cared for by Edwina and Charles. He was soon to be valued as treasurer of the Sports and Social Club and Priory Club and his keen interest in village affairs continued. His able brain and remarkable memory capably linked the present with the past so that his contribution to the little booklet to be published will make it unique and Herbert Wing remembered as a respected son of Southwick.

www.ingramcontent.com/pod-product-compliance
Lightning Source LLC
Chambersburg PA
CBHW071038080526
44587CB00015B/2667